SPOTTING DIFFERENCES

Butterfly or Moth?

by Christina Leaf

BLASTOFF! READERS

BELLWETHER MEDIA • MINNEAPOLIS, MN

Note to Librarians, Teachers, and Parents:

Blastoff! Readers are carefully developed by literacy experts and combine standards-based content with developmentally appropriate text.

Level 1 provides the most support through repetition of high-frequency words, light text, predictable sentence patterns, and strong visual support.

Level 2 offers early readers a bit more challenge through varied simple sentences, increased text load, and less repetition of high-frequency words.

Level 3 advances early-fluent readers toward fluency through increased text and concept load, less reliance on visuals, longer sentences, and more literary language.

Level 4 builds reading stamina by providing more text per page, increased use of punctuation, greater variation in sentence patterns, and increasingly challenging vocabulary.

Level 5 encourages children to move from "learning to read" to "reading to learn" by providing even more text, varied writing styles, and less familiar topics.

Whichever book is right for your reader, Blastoff! Readers are the perfect books to build confidence and encourage a love of reading that will last a lifetime!

This edition first published in 2020 by Bellwether Media, Inc.

No part of this publication may be reproduced in whole or in part without written permission of the publisher. For information regarding permission, write to Bellwether Media, Inc., Attention: Permissions Department, 6012 Blue Circle Drive, Minnetonka, MN 55343.

Library of Congress Cataloging-in-Publication Data

Names: Leaf, Christina, author.
Title: Butterfly or Moth? / by Christina Leaf.
Description: Minneapolis, MN : Bellwether Media, Inc., [2020] | Series: Blastoff! Readers: Spotting Differences | Audience: Age 5-8. | Audience: K to Grade 3. | Includes bibliographical references and index.
Identifiers: LCCN 2018054608 (print) | LCCN 2018056488 (ebook) | ISBN 9781618915733 (ebook) | ISBN 9781644870327 (hardcover : alk. paper)
Subjects: LCSH: Butterflies--Juvenile literature. | Moths--Juvenile literature.
Classification: LCC QL544.2 (ebook) | LCC QL544.2 .L435 2020 (print) | DDC 595.78/9--dc23
LC record available at https://lccn.loc.gov/2018054608

Editor: Al Albertson   Designer: Jeffrey Kollock

Printed in the United States of America, North Mankato, MN.

Table of Contents

Butterflies and Moths

Butterflies and moths are both beautiful **insects**. They have big wings.

moth

These insects are
close cousins.
How can you tell
which is which?

butterfly

The insects have different looks. Most moth wings have dull colors. Butterfly wings are bright!

butterfly wing

Butterfly **antennae** are shaped like clubs. Moth antennae look like **combs**.

moth antennae

butterfly antennae

Butterflies are
bigger than moths.
Some are 1 foot
(30.5 centimeters) wide!

Different Lives

The insects act differently. Moths rest with their wings spread out. Butterflies hold them up.

14

Moths curl up in **cocoons** to grow. Butterflies grow up in hard **chrysalises**.

chrysalis

cocoon

Butterflies take
flight in the day.
Moths fly at night.
Which insect is this?

club-tipped
antennae

colorful
wings

larger size

Butterfly Differences

fly during
the day

hold their
wings up

grow in
chrysalises

feathery
antennae

dull-colored
wings

smaller size

Moth Differences

fly during
the night

hold their
wings out

grow in
cocoons

21

Glossary

antennae

feelers connected to the head that sense information around them

combs

small tools with many teeth that are used to get knots out of hair

chrysalises

hard shells that form around caterpillars while they change into butterflies

insects

small animals with six legs and hard outer bodies

cocoons

silk cases that young moths spin around themselves for safety while they grow

To Learn More

AT THE LIBRARY

Feltwell, John. *Butterflies and Moths*. New York, N.Y.: DK/Penguin Random House, 2018.

Leaf, Christina. *Butterflies*. Minneapolis, Minn.: Bellwether Media, 2018.

Perish, Patrick. *Moths*. Minneapolis, Minn.: Bellwether Media, 2018.

ON THE WEB

FACTSURFER

Factsurfer.com gives you a safe, fun way to find more information.

1. Go to www.factsurfer.com.

2. Enter "butterfly or moth" into the search box and click 🔍.

3. Select your book cover to see a list of related web sites.

Index

The images in this book are reproduced through the courtesy of: anek.soowannaphoom, front cover (butterfly); iliuta goean, front cover (moth); RudiErnst, pp. 4-5; Kemal ATLI, pp. 6-7; Henrik Larsson, pp. 8-9; KRIACHKO OLEKSII, p. 9 (butterfly wing); Paijoedirt, pp. 10-11; TSN52, p. 11 (butterfly); MassimilianoDoria, iStock, pp. 12-13; David Havel, pp. 14-15; tcareob72, pp. 16-17; hrui, p. 17 (cocoon); Lovely Bird, pp. 18-19; anusorn2005, p. 20 (butterfly); Songdech Kothmongkol, p. 20 (daylight); Sean Xu, p. 20 (butterfly wings); Stephane Bidouze, p. 20 (chrysalis); Wanida_Sri, p. 21 (moth); Ilkin Zeferli, p. 21 (night); Kluciar Ivan, p. 21 (moth wings); Landshark1, p. 21 (cocoon); guraydere, p. 22 (antennae); Leena Robinson, p. 22 (chrysalis); Matt Jeppson, p.22 (cocoon); Alex Oakenman, p. 22 (comb); frank60, p. 22 (insects).